"The corner-corner boy of me that picks
Away at the corner of things!

I could, instead, make myself remarkable,
And plain lunatic, for you"

Highlife for Caliban (Lemuel Johnson)

ALONG THE ODOKOKO RIVER

AHMED KOROMA

With poems from

"Of Flour and Tears"

Along the Odokoko River
Copyright © 2016 by Ahmed Koroma
All rights reserved.

ISBN: 978-99910-54-43-8

Sierra Leonean Writers Series

For Ramatu, Majeed and Zara

Table of Contents

Foreword by Mohamed Gibril Sesay …………….. 1

REFLECTION

Freedom…………………………………………	11
Dreams………………………………………….	12
Fly Away…………………………………………	13
Soliloquy………………………………………….	15
Easter………………………………………….	16
Revelation………………………………………...	17
Offering………………………………………….	18
Rebranding……………………………………..	19
Dark Clouds…………………………………....	20
The Rebirth of Salioko……………………………	21
Home…………………………………………..	22
Dear River……………………………………...	24
Limbo of the Patriarch……………………………	25
Ebenezer……………………………………….	26
Diamonds……………………………………..	27
Resilience……………………………………...	28
Odokoko Flow………………………………...	29
Odokoko Blues………………………………..	30
Silhouette………………………………………	32
Where Four Roads Meet………………………….	33

REFRACTION

Underneath the Sky…………………………………	35
A Poet's Life…………………………………………..	36
Gesture………………………………………………...	37
Deserted………………………………………………	38
Pathway………………………………………………	39
Ponder…………………………………………………	40
At the Waterside……………………………………..	41
Innocence Lost……………………………………..	42
Dark Skin……………………………………………	43
Memory………………………………………………	44

OF FLOUR AND TEARS   45

Afterword by Kayode R. Robbin-Coker ………   91

Yearning for a Mermaid

Foreword by

Mohamed Gibril Sesay

Ahmed Koroma's poetry shows his love for a city of rivers, rains, rocks and childhood, and he yearns for it. The title of this collection, *Along the Odokoko River*, refers to a waterway that runs right through the middle of this city, meandering from the hilly boulders of its South to the rocky shorelines of its Atlantic. The city is Freetown, Sierra Leone. The hills of Freetown are majestic, but the poet is not concerned with them. Rather he hugs the flow, the movement, and the freedom of that central waterway of a city founded and dedicated to the pursuit of freedom. Ahmed Koroma shows great fidelity to this central ideal of Freetown - 'let me roam free' he cries in the very first poem of the collection.

The poet's vision is also inspired by the spiritual landscapes of his childhood – the Muslim *adhan* or call to prayer, the kites of Easter, the legend of *Salioko*; these reveal the contrapuntal but melding spirituality and metaphoric accents of a person who grew up in the Central and East End crannies of Freetown. His loyalty to these lands bordering the East and West bank of the *Odokoko* is not in doubt:

> *We remain loyal to this part of town*
> *We impatiently await the eerie moment*

A spirit of waiting runs through these poems, albeit active waiting, as seen in the poem 'Dreams'. Here the poet reiterates his love for freedom, a type that is contingent on his head, resting on the shiny boulders of his childhood:

So it is with mixed feeling that I come here
To rest my head against the slimy boulders
To dream away, and then wait for the rain to fall

The poem 'Fly Away' tells us about a bird, 'ambitious and wild', but which 'feels my pain'. It is as if the poet's pain here is that of a person whose body is stuck where his spirit has left. In 'Easter', this tragic-beautiful weaving of contradictions looms; even though the small bodies of Freetown's children couldn't fly, their dreams, their kites all over the skies of Easter Freetown, would ascend unto freedom after they had disgraced the Judases betraying their salvation:

When we yell and hold tight to a bundle of thread
When we silently wish we could fly away in zest
We let our kites sail through the evening instead

The theme of 'freedom but being stuck' and the pain of this situation are evident in another poem, 'Rebrand'. The pendulum of our poet's metaphors often swings from some gain to pain, movement (along the *Odokoko*), an earthy waterway, to waiting for rain from the heavens. In the poem 'Soliloquy' we see the poet making a move, but he is still waiting for an answer:

> *While I anticipate a much needed encore*
> *It is with assorted emotions*
> *That I continue to wait by the shore*

He is not passive in that sense. The other side lures him, he makes his move, but the other side refrains from coming to him, 'so he 'lust(s) for [her] return'. It is almost as if the poet longs to return to something that is no longer there, but the longing moves him, so he 'continue(s) to wait by the shore'.

And in the poem '*Odokoko Blues*,' the poet's expectation is evident: 'I wish for your return', he wants his dreams unchained, he wants to 'leap over the course of the embankment' *(Odokoko Flow)*; 'my heart bleeds for your return' (*Silhouette*).

Freetown is a city of rains; the seasonal joy of playing in the rain is an indelible part of male childhood. The poet is a lover of rain. In *'Dark Clouds'*, he writes:

> *The hurrying clouds surge across the sky*
> *With no counting stars to form a plough*
> *And no lazy moon to lend its shine*
>
> *So we dance and dance to the gusty wind*
> *And patiently wait for the rain to begin*
> *It's been a while since we had a drenching one*

Rain is his symbol of hope, of freedom, of the joys of childhood. The poet speaks of home as a return unto 'where heavy rain falls on green slimy rock.' Home, he writes, is 'my childhood nest.' In the poem '*Ebenezer*', he writes, 'our childhood place that we call home.' It is this childhood, this resilience of the sweet memories that is blossoming into these fine poems. This is what we get in the poem '*Resilience;*'

The resilience of this memory of love
The seeds that fell on fertile ground
Thrived at last, underneath a bamboo shade

But there are seeds that fell on infertile lands, or efforts that seem infertile. This seems to be the case with efforts relating to diamonds. Hardly, any Sierra Leonean writes without mentioning diamonds, and the grim fate this precious stone has bestowed on the nation. In the poem, '*Diamonds*' our poet writes about the hazards of seeking wealth through diamonds and its toll on the country's body. The poet almost utters a prayer for a halt to this nihilistic destiny of the citizen who may 'toil the earth until the day/The molten iron finally chars him away.' This sort of nihilistic possibility is weaved into a number of poems – movement tugged at by waiting; dreams tethered unto boulders; 'large rocks resist[ing] your gushiness;' and as we see in the very first poem of the collection, the celebratory self-plucking of one's wings, as if freely travelling to a place where the means of flight, of freedom, is destroyed in itself the essence of the journey.

The Collection is divided into two sections: *Reflection*, which covers the first part and what we have been discussing so far, and the second section, *Refraction*. But even in the section he calls *Refraction,* we follow the poet's vision and re-vision travelling along different wavelengths. He travels through varying mediums – his experiences, his recalling of them, the metaphors of a multiple heritage; the collection is a collage of heritage - Islamic, Christian, the pantheon of the Yoruba Arisha, and the exilic conditions of

Along the Odokoko River

his longings (he currently lives in California). But though the wavelengths may be travelling at different speeds or at varying angles, the poet succeeds in weaving them into a perceptible and empathic vision for us through the universal human themes of longing, waiting, freedom, and the everlasting marks of childhood.

The poems in *'Reflection'* are more or less communal encounters, whilst those in *Refraction* are mostly about one to one encounters, or lack therefore of, between the poet and some other single existence that he yearns. In the poem 'Underneath the Stars,' the poet uses metaphors and words that suggest what Freetown resident's would refer to as 'Mami Water', the lady of the sea, beautiful, enticing, dangerous, a femme fatale. But the poet transforms the emerging vision into the lady of his dreams:

'I see you in my dreams, many nights
Your palms and heels painted in black
Clad in a single cloth with colorful prints'.

But the poet's longing is unrequited, 'Oblivious to the voiceless songs I sing.' One is reminded of a childhood crush that one is too much of a coward or shy person to speak ones heart to. So the search continues, the vision of the beautiful is sustained, but it too often dimmed by the mundane:

'...the madding crowd interrupts my vision
While calling for roasted cassava and corn'

In the next poem, the *'A Poets Life,'* the poet describes his life as if it is one of fighting against this descent into the nothingness of the mundane, and he can only halt this descent by pinning down his dreams.

'If I didn't reach out for a crumpled paper
And scribble rubbish and save for later
As I scramble away to grasp at saneness
I would be overrun by nothingness.'

This effort is almost a Sisyphus like toil of rolling boulders of metaphors over and over again. But this was/is/will be the toil, as he suggests in the poem, *'Gesture,'* make him feel '…the adoring link/For the very first time/I sensed a synaptic feeling /That transforms a simple gesture /Into a moment of magic/That seems to last forever.

But don't be fooled by it, it does not last forever. The poet in fact does not want it to last forever, for the yearning is sweeter than the fulfilling:

'I did not want to let go
But I am glad I did
For now I long for more
When you unhurriedly pull away'

Whilst it is insightful to suggest that the poet paints childhoods of joys, we also get a glimpse of some childhoods of pain, of desertion. And it is instructive to note that the childhood the poet gives this pain to, is that of a girl, 'A hapless girl with a cross to bear.' Is the poem *'Desertion'* a cry against the discriminations against girls in our societies? As is the case with most of the poems in this section, this is about a person-to-person encounter, about 'a little girl with memories and lasting scar/A forsaken child with a broken past.' But these encounters could well be refractions of wavelengths upon wavelengths of collective abuse into a perceptible whole made possible by the poet's empathic rendering.

Empathic renditions ensure a collection, so to speak, that is not flat, or that are sediments of the same color, a collection of only one way of looking of phenomena. Rather, we have a collection that has roundness, fullness, and humanity in its splendor of varied circumstances. In 'Pathway,' we see another view of girlhood in our parts:

'With a twinkle smile on her oily face
With a reflection of a mother
Who has waited for this day.'

These metaphors of our land describe the elegant particulars of this girl. 'Her trinkets around her contoured neck/Shines bright against her polished dark skin/Dangling bells of a colorful masquerade.'

These are descriptions of beauty that could easily be understood by persons socialized into the aesthetic metaphors of our land, Freetown, Sierra Leone, Africa. But many of the metaphors have a more restrictive range – Central and East End Freetown, Kaibara, Bambra Tong, and Fula Tong, where the poet had his childhood experience. But the poet's empathic orientations make it easy to translate, or even transplant these accents, these unique versifications, into universal insights.

Let me explain this in relation to the poem *'Ponder'*. This poem is a call to dreams that utilizes the experiential and mythic resources of the East and West banks of the *Odokoko*:

Ahmed Koroma

Allow the pounding of the slanted rain
On rusty corrugated zinc wall
To ponder your thoughts away

What language!!! Definitely, rains in Freetown are slanted, they never come down straight, but curved like its mountains and streams, 'a sobering place/Where jinns and men collide.' It was one such collision, in my mind, that led the Freetown Peninsula to be called by some Portuguese Sierra Lyoa, the Lion Mountain, which later collided with English accents to become Sierra Leone, giving birth to another collision that got Sierra Leoneans to popularly call their land Salone. Tales of jinns, of their collisions with men and women emblazon the conversations of the people at the banks of the *Odokoko*, and these jinns are variously called *jinna*, and *debul* and could be both malevolent and benevolent.

In this collection, the poet mostly avoids writing about the politics of the land and the despoliations of war, themes that tend to dominate the accents of most of the country's poets of his generation. But even at that, we glimpse in the poem *'Innocence Lost'*, that the poet does not trust the makers of (political) promises. And in the poem, *'Salioko'* he utilizes allusion to the Yoruba Orishas, an allusion that many along the banks of the *Odokoko* would relate to, to speak of rebirth after war. Ahmed Koroma has given us a collection that utilizes the accents of the Freetown that borders the *Odokoko* to speak the universality of longing and dreaming.

In *Dark Skin*, the poet fights to remain himself, a Freetown man with expansive empathy, who is giving us palimpsest of multiple heritages. He understands the contours of struggle, its promise and pitfalls, its telling and muting, and this he reveals in the last poem of this collection, '*Memory.*' Here the poet tells us of struggles of yore that on the face of it look like wasted efforts, but which also carries hope that future generations would not have to waste efforts fighting injustice, for justice would have been the taken-for-granted backdrop of human endeavors.

Having read this empathic work of memory, I tried to coin a word or phrase, a singularity that would explain this collection, a sort of explanation made simple, which the wise-talking persons of the junctions of East End Freetown would use to describe it to the world. I vote for the Krio word 'yan'. Yan in Krio means 'to woo,' its etymology suggests the English word yearn, which tells us about longing. The marriage of the meanings of these two words suggests longing, which one may see as passive, and also wooing which makes it active. The collection shows some active waiting, resilient longing, movement, dreams that are at the same time sleepy and active, a great dance of the soul.

Ahmed Koroma

REFLECTION

Along the Odokoko River

Freedom

Do not tell me where to tread
Let me wander into wilderness
Anytime, any day as I please

Let me roam free around the green
Stroking the petals of hibiscus
And yellow and purple allamanda
Let me be reckless in my expressiveness
And my freedom to live the life I choose

Do not guide me through my rambling
Let me sing the blues and fly away
Beyond yonder into a faraway land

For later I will pluck my wings and retire well
Into the night, with those who have walked this path
This route lined by thorns and weeds
This shore of roses where we plan to meet
So you can tread and ramble like me

Dreams

I have dreams to fulfill
Those that I left to marinate in a half-filled bowl

So as I breathe colorless pungent air,
Sliding down slippery rocks
Head first, and tumbling into the spring
My spirit floats in this trance
My soulfulness flanking on nirvana

Dreams
The escape route into passive space
Which I prefer to my waking days
Along the riverbanks

So it is with mixed feeling that I come here
To rest my head against the slimy boulders
To dream away, and then wait for the rain to fall

Fly Away

*"There will be no love that's dying here
the bird that flew in through my window
simply lost his way."*

Gregory Porter (No Love Dying)

The bird that flew in through my window

She must have flown alone
Away from the flock
A bird so bold
So seemingly out of luck
But unflinching and purposeful
And hard as a rock
She flew back from the pane
Where she was stuck

The bird that flew in through my window

Ambitious and wild,
Unafraid of her past
This bird took heed
When the die is cast
She will fly through the rainbow,
She will fly back
She had taken refuge at my abode,
But it wasn't to last

The bird that flew in through my window

Ahmed Koroma

A dove that sail into the yonder sky
A purposeful wanderer,
A soulful bird

She did lose her way
And she was avoiding the rain
She is flying away,
And she is feeling my pain

Soliloquy

So it is with assorted emotions
That I continue to wait by the shore
Hoping for you to hurriedly turn back
To serenade me once again
With that sonorous pitch

A queen of the river you are
Evident in your grand pageantry
From last night's sail downstream
Your glitters match the stars
And the broken bottles beside my feet

So as I lust for your return
And refuse the curtain call
While I anticipate a much needed encore
It is with assorted emotions
That I continue to wait by the shore

Ahmed Koroma

Easter

It is with hope that we traverse this shoddy path
The rise of the spirit from the running stream
As we have done many moons in the past

We should have known this day would come
We had wished for this in our restless slumber
After we killed Judas a million times over

So as we watch our kites dangle in the air
Boundlessly, tailless, as they drift away slowly
From the riverbank where we jubilantly cheer

When we yell and hold tight to a bundle of thread
When we silently wish we could fly away in zest
We let our kites sail through the evening instead

Along the Odokoko River

Revelation

We play castaways along the riverbanks
Abandoned by white horses and ghosts
Because we choose to read the apostle's creed
And count rosaries as we please

It is with trepidation when we ponder
About the apocalypse, of the after world
Wishing we were still drifting in circles

But we are left to tread along
This cold path in meditation
After we plunge into stupor

As we remain loyal to this part of town
We impatiently await the eerie moment
When white horses and ghosts reappear

So we chase wild rodents around the creek
Anticipating the *adhan* call from the minaret
Before performing a hurried *alwala*[1]

We will then sail back to the waterfall
To receive our rosaries and prayer mats
And to salute the *jinns* as they ascend slowly
Through the blue smoke into the *Samaa'a*[2]

---

[1] An ablution before a Muslim prayer
[2] *Samaa'a* – The skies (samawat (pl.)) – in Arabic refers to the visible sky as referenced in verses in the Quran, implying the Heavens. The words samaa'a/samawat occur over 300 times in the Qur'an

Ahmed Koroma

Offering

Let us roll rims of steel across a tiny bridge
And scream the names of our rebellious friends
Those unafraid to chase hairless dogs
Down and underneath the bridge
Into the stream where blue water flows

This is the day the town healer howls all day
When we gather around him with clasped hands
Crossed legs across a large cotton sheet
Staring at copper coins shiny on top of kola nuts
Awaiting his supplication on behalf of a sick child

We gaze at rice bowls and buried steaming soup
A concatenation of thoughts, a laughter betrayed
Because we are told to shut our little eyes
And silently recite Surat al ikhlas seven times
Lest *Shai'tan*[3] snatches away our little hearts

The healer hums a tune and performs exorcism
Over and over again with a mirror in his hand
So what do we gain from going round in circles
And singing canticles and hymns in the churchyards?
What do we see when we are so blindfolded?

We cheer in jubilation when the sick child smiles
And then drink dirty concoctions from stained cups
That the healer passes around after his incantations
After he tosses the potpourri of yesterday's sacrifice
In the river as a ritual for those who departed

---

[3] Shai'tan, Satan.

Rebranding

With a torn flag, he runs a lap
Around the ramparts of the edifice
The one the colonialists built
The one that was made to last

Tell him more lies he can believe
Make him celebrate his independence
And then let him prostrate at your door
For you to come back and rescue his poor

The relic of the war remains with us
So we whitewash the bloodstained walls
And paint over the scars from the wound
But scavenge around looking for food

Let him continue to dance the hunters' dance
And wave the mast above the wailing crowd
It's a new world, a beginning, a newer day
And no one will take his happiness away

The unpreparedness for the next fight
The one that wilts the blossom flowers
And slowly reveals the patched cracks
Catapulting all of us back to our very past

Ahmed Koroma

Dark Clouds

We laze beside the stream detached
Witnessing the hovering dark clouds' flight
And the intermittent thundering roar of the night

The elation as we await the drenching rain
The hail that grudgingly refuses to fall
The one we are sternly warned to avoid

But why should we be afraid of a storm?
That descends tonight with its might and force
Why should dark clouds make us run?

The hurrying clouds surge across the sky
With no counting stars to form a plough
And no lazy moon to lend its shine

So we dance and dance to the gusty wind
And patiently wait for the rain to begin
It's been a while since we had a drenching one

Along the Odokoko River

The Rebirth of Salioko

Ogun retreats and sheathes his hammer
His weapon of truth, the one he wields
When water splashes around the creek
The day the marauders invade our town
And people run for the overlooking hills

He is our warrior king
The protector, our wing

He was *Tobe Ode* [4]
Before coming to the creek
As he sprung out from the body of the queen

So give him palm oil and chicken feet
Let us wipe our hands on his knees

Give him pounded yam and cooked beans
For we welcome him home again
After the bloody battle is won

Give him ginger and kola nut
Let him spit the chaff at the junction
And into the mouth of the newborn
For life triumphs, and once again
Salioko celebrates him with drums

---

[4] Ogun is a primordial Orisha whose first appearance was as a hunter named Tobe Ode.

Ahmed Koroma

Home

Take me back to my distant abode
Where heavy rain falls on green slimy rocks
And dew on shoreline cocoyam leaves
At dawn before the *adhan* call
I think of the mistiness of my dwelling place
And the gloomy clouds hovering over me
I think of the waterfall that carries the tune
Of the boy whose whistling reverberates
As he beats his drum in readiness
And then sing songs to observe *Rabi' al-awwal* [5]

It brings me back to my wholesomeness
And the longing to revert to my childhood nest

Take me back to my place of yearning
Where wandering, abandoned dogs retreat
And the stray cat with piercing eyes
Startles and stares through the moonless night
The putridness and stale carcass
Of my decomposed melancholy
As I long to go back to my very past
Reawaken my eagerness to make that journey
To the cobbler who mends my beleaguered soul

It brings me back to my wholesomeness
And the longing to revert to my childhood nest

---

[5] The third month in the Islamic calendar during which some Muslims celebrate *Mawlid* - the birthday of the Islamic prophet Muhammad

Along the Odokoko River

Take me back to the home where I belong
Where evading mosquitos return a tune
An ode to muffled ears and mucus filled nose
The place I covet, the place I wish I never left
Where my umbilical cord is buried underneath
A leaning banana tree, buried in fecal mess
Amidst the cacophony of trading wares
At the junction where four roads meet
Where my irksome moment is transformed
Into bliss with the aroma of a sidewalk vendor

It brings me back to my wholesomeness
And the longing to revert to my childhood nest

Dear River

Dear River
You passed me by last night
As I sat on this algae laden rock
And I wondered if I should flow with you.

Let the twinkle in my eyes
Squeeze some tears
That will accompany you,
On your journey
When you pass me by next time

I watch you pass me by everyday
And I wonder if you know my name
Or hear our heart beats

Let the sorrow that hangs over me
Drowns itself on your banks,
And sail along with you
When you pass me by next time

When you swell and gush
Past our abode at night
And the large rocks resist your gushiness
My mind wanders with you too

Let the pebbles that get washed
Downstream by your might
And the debris that floats on your back
Take that journey for me

Limbo of the Patriarchs

"I came to this land of Kutuje
To see for myself
The truth of the rumoured wailings..."
Ola Rotimi, The Gods Are Not to Blame

The rock we pound our clothes on
By the waterside
Will cleanse our soul at dawn
For last night
At Dante's peak
Up against the Iroko tree
We witnessed the red-hot lava gushing upwards,
After we waved our white cloths for peace
After the marauders and the plunderers
Had ransacked and pillaged our village paths
We faded away, unhurriedly
But we came back after the storm
After the swarming bees had drifted away
To drink lemongrass, tea-bush
And ginger beer

Ebenezer

The stone we cherish, the Azteca block
The one we chose as the cornerstone rock

It rests effortlessly on the corner wall
Revered by pilgrims who've answered the call

So when the chorister lustily sings a hymn
He would stretch his arm to praise the king

And the old man who walks towards the pew
To read the plaque, the names of the few

Those who have past through the sanctuary door
Those ones to whom we dedicate His word

He would bow his head and close his eyes
And whisper a prayer to shed all vice

This gate, wide open for us to roam
Our childhood place that we call our home

It was below the hill amid the city noise
Our voices quivered as we prayed for all

Along the Odokoko River

Diamonds

He is in search of a precious mineral
Instead is scorched by molten iron
Underneath the burning sun

He would rather reach for a different ore
A simple one in another muddy soil
But he continues to shake and toggle his sieve
Looking for earth's little jewel within

A prostrating lizard watches on
His every bend, his grunt and toil
Sweat dripping from his bushy eyebrow
Grime positioning on his protruding temple
Wrinkle, a path on his contoured face

Would the unforgiving earth be so gentle
Than to spare him a tiny rock
Or would he toil the earth until the day
The molten iron finally chars him away

Ahmed Koroma

Resilience

Those seeds that fell on fertile ground
Watered and nourished, but refusing to grow

But we later watch them sprout along the banks
After the last cloudburst that drenched the town
The one that drowned the beggar with the broken heart

The days were longer than the nights
So we sat down by the blossom flowers
And counted pebbles that we threw into the air

The resilience of this memory of love
Those seeds that fell on fertile ground
Thrived at last, underneath a bamboo shade

Odokoko Blues

The lullabies you whisper to me
As you dance around the fireside
Around the creek where red water flows
Place me in a state of contemplation

You sing sweet melodies to me
Your voice echoing around the hollowed pass
Bouncing of clay walls and houses on stilts
Among croaking toads and earthworms

When you sing the final tune to me
And walk your way into the smoke
And then hurriedly dash into the night
I wish for your return

So your departure after the storm
After the bonfire ashes circles away
Left a vacuum that sucks the air around me
At the place where red water flows

Ahmed Koroma

Odokoko Flow

Unchain my dream
Let me walk freely through the crowd
Until I find my solace, my bliss
My goal and my purpose to live
Freedom to dream, to become, to pursue
Freedom to live the life we choose
Not to be bogged down by those who rule
And to think of us as wretched fools
Salivating over their goods and pillaged loot

Unchain my vision
Let me walk on water like I used to
For I was born and raised along this flow
Tiptoed over its course on jagged rocks
Survived the flood, the red water gush
Never afraid of the deluge, or another rush
Are we not the children you left to rot?
To fend for bread while you cruised in trucks
Should we display the scars and the burns?
The paths we took and the uneven turns

Unchain my future
So I can unravel myself from your fettered grip
And run not stand on my own two feet
This river seems shallow but it is so deep
And I'm raring to go for that desperate leap
Over the course of the embankment I hurry
Tripping but readily rise again not tarry
My dream realized in spite of your roadblocks

Along the Odokoko River

My determination to reach the top is no luck
For a desire to win back my dream at all cost

Ahmed Koroma

Silhouette

If silence is the language you speak
Humming of birds overhead your echo
Of the wonderful songs you sing
If darkness represents your beauty
Your movement, your motionless walk
Down the riverbed among snails

And when you threw that veil over your face
To become your elusive silhouette self
It was then that I felt your boldness
An audacity that shattered my comprehension

For your silkiness and the wetness of your hair
And the euphony of your majestic sail
Vindicate my brief sojourn at the riverbanks
And my hearts bleeds for your return

Along the Odokoko River

Where Four Roads Meet

He cuddles a pint
The one he nurses all day long
As the merengue music belches through
The bug infested wooden speaker

This is our hodgepodge junction
Where four roads meet
Where many souls convene
A bright spot in a dark town

A Makiadi[6] song takes its turn
And the performer swings in tune
He must have motioned the bartender
To switch the tempo up a bit

A rendezvous for the dejected
And the powerbrokers as well
But the performer is oblivious to this
If you care not to dance with him

---

[6] François Luambo Luanzo Makiadi (6 July 1938 – 12 October 1989) was a major figure in twentieth century Congolese music, and African music in general.

Ahmed Koroma

REFRACTION

Underneath the Stars

I see you in my dreams, many nights
As I lie down underneath the stars
Down at the river
I see you sail downstream
Unbothered by the raging water
And the drifting rafts
I long to see you when I'm awake,
But rather it is the translucent image
Of cowries dangling in your wavy hair

I see you in my dreams, many nights
Your palms and heels painted in black
Clad in a single cloth with colorful prints
Oblivious to the voiceless songs I sing
For last night as I laid down beside the rocks
When the madding crowd interrupts my vision
While calling for roasted cassava and corn
It was the first time I pictured you
A soul in search of a soulful mate

Ahmed Koroma

A Poet's Life

If I didn't put words down to paper last night
After awakening from a delirious nightmare
Down at the riverside
If I didn't reach out for a rumpled paper
And scribble rubbish and save for later
As I scramble away to grasp at saneness
I would be overrun by nothingness

Words. Big words. Floating words
Circumnavigating around a peripheral
Disjointed words, no sense words.
Perched and sometimes dangling inside
Anticlockwise spins, nonconforming dream
Sleuthing lyrics, furious disputing rhythms
Dissonant verses declining to be conquered

If I didn't put words on paper last night
Sewing verses, my imprisoned moment
Entropies of stanzas, hitherto disjointed
I jotted down as fast as I could remember
To journey back to my awaiting slumber
It is a poet's life; a welcomed unending trance

Gesture

When I held your hand last night
I felt the adoring link
For the very first time
I sensed a synaptic feeling
That transformed a simple gesture
Into a moment of magic
That seemed to last forever.

When I held your hand last night
I did not want to let go
But I am glad I did
For now I long for more
When you unhurriedly pull away

When I held your hand last night
My hand eclipsing yours
It was like a fantasy dream
A moment of magic
That will surely last forever

Ahmed Koroma

Deserted

You gingerly walk past my door
Sometimes late at night
Other times early in the morn

A grimace on your face
A smile, a grin and often a gaze
A hapless girl with a cross to bear

You friskily hopscotch your way back
A little girl with memories and lasting scar
A forsaken child with a broken past

Pathway

The child who walks through a rocky way
With a twinkle smile on her oily face
With a reflection of a mother
Who has waited for this day
Tells the story of a past
A present and an unending path

Her trinkets around her contoured neck
Shines bright against her polished dark skin
Dangling bells of a colorful masquerade
Accompanies the child as she walks her path

She will be smiling too
The day her daughter walks this path again
Like her mother and grandmother
And all those who came before her

Ahmed Koroma

Ponder

Dream if you can

Allow the gust of the wind to take your mind
Into a sobering place
Where jinns and men collide

Let your emotions cascade
Into a smoke-filled room
On top of a caravan of flies

Allow the pounding of the slanted rain
On rusty corrugated zinc wall
To ponder your thoughts away

Along the Odokoko River

At the waterside

She leans, whispers and playfully nudges
She must have missed that moment of magic
The moments we spent by the waterside
Where splashes of water pound on uneven rocks
Reminding her of those olden days of yore

It is the hold, the touch, and the walk to the edge
Of the waterfall. It is the mistiness, the moon
That follows us through grassy trail
Amid the slowly moving clouds
As we navigate around the stream

It is the banging of pans, the ant lines I see
That is distracting me
And her aroma, her strength and her smile
So she nudges me again, a sweet elbow shove
Reminding me of what I have missed all those years.

Ahmed Koroma

Innocence Lost

I do not trust your commitment
To rescue those who sleep on cracked sidewalk
Mildewed and left to rot
During their formative years

I cannot comprehend the vindication
Of those who placed guns in the hands
Of the man child
Who misses many years of education

I will not acknowledge your unstructured plans
To assist the kids in the slum
Who have been neglected over the years
While you retreat to the grassy hilltop

So it is with great apprehension
That I take that journey back to a land
Where crocodiles eat their young
And celebrate them for many years to come

Dark Skin

I do not want you to destroy my dark skin
With the sharp edges of your fingernails
To extinguish my dream, my melanin
With your apathy and brute force
I do not want you to pull me back
To whitewash my stream of thoughts
Nor reap my skin of its pigmentation
My blackness that represents perseverance

As you attempt to negate my dreams
With senselessness and vanity
I choose to detach from your absurdity
I prefer to bask under the equatorial sun
With reinforced spirit to win at all cost
So I yearn for those days of yore
When my skin was darker than ore
And my determination to live and explore
Was larger than my battle scars

Memory

The old man steadfastly stands his ground
Against the invading hordes
Who have chosen to make their voices heard
As he did in his youthful days
So he soars above the wobbly bridge
Unbothered by the riotous chant
Those who have come to make their mark
And express grievance like the ones in the past
The old man is not going to walk away
As he sniffs the toxic pungent teargas
It is a nostalgic feeling he thinks
For he no longer throws Molotov cocktail
Like he did his against the Tonton Macoutes
Many moons ago
So he silently watches the crowd
Burying his head into his hands
And wish the next generation
Wouldn't have to face this crisis again

Along the Odokoko River

OF FLOUR AND TEARS

Prelude (the smoke)

Ahmed Koroma

Rain

the mud-splashing and the drizzle of today
left me pondering about my yesterdays

at the merry-go round, we were unclad kids
sailing in the overflowing stream
away from the akosombo dam

but red water came gushing
and this intoxicating smell of rain
blended well with elephant grass and tea bush

the breeze and lightening, we danced the samba
though last night my ears were covered
with grandma's quilt when the thunder roared

the mud-splashing, the drizzle of today
left me pondering about my yesterdays

The Red Sun

its redness penetrates the grayish clouds
with westerly wind racing toward the rocky hills

a hungry stomach, a duodenal bacterium, waiting out
a breakfast meal, a maggot feast the rays will bring

but we stay all night; witness the red anopheles' flight
with strained eyes we now see the tired moon

when the sun is awake we'll play hide and seek
we will sing a song, we will fret no gloom

but the warning sign, we dare not look at him
lest the redness follows the eyes that never sleep

this sun blinds those that dare to dream
those with zest and fervor, those unafraid to speak

Ahmed Koroma

The Bridge

a cave, decorated
with stalactites and stalagmites
where wet snails
are embedded in clayey rocks
and where cow skins
are soaked in burgundy dyes
all through the night.

the bridge will not fall tonight
but my heaving heart has melted away

across the stream
we follow the cow dung trail
while skipping through puddles
and dry excreta

tomorrow, the bridge will tremble and fall
and my feet will give way to the resonant force

Prayer

the saturated mixture of flour and tears
the expectation from all these years

did my people pray their lives away
while satan's maniacal laugh echoes
outside the minaret walls
I watch them
as they head for the bridge
because the mosque could not hold them all
they pray over and over
(under and over the bridge)
even the catholics come
to read the apostle's creed
I watch them
as they walk to the park
their white *agbada* sweeping dust

they pray over and over
even the *adejohbis* do
(and the agnostics too)
they roll and speak in tongues

the saturated mixture of flour and tears
the expectation from all these years

Ahmed Koroma

In-Dependence

the tears from my eyes

as I weep blood, colorless blood
and dance bare-footed while raising dust

I ponder

what species eat their young at birth
and celebrate the birthdays of years to come

the jubilation last night
our deliberate mental block
of why we celebrate our independence

Is it the love for our motherland
our freedom from shackles
vise on our ankles

Is it our mind, being decolonized
our transient divorce overnight

what independence

but we celebrate

Tower Hill

the reservoir holds enough
to drown the town
but we wash our faces upwards
defying the odds
singing lullaby to aging grandparents
while riding on naked tires towards the stream.

our red ribbons tied firmly
around our wrist
as we swim down the water course for
yellow woman won't scare us at noon

but our suffocated nostrils
smell of dry blood from carcass of rats

those halcyon days, in the morning
we played with *gbetas* filled with pebbles
and crushed metal cups

but we return
after high noon, after the pulpit call
to kill Judas
and celebrate with pig feet and dry roots

Ahmed Koroma

The Mad Man
(from east end freetown)

he speaks
softly, incoherently,
deliberately chewing white chalk
while writing equations
on the side walk
to solve global destituteness
once and for all

he sips
hot soup for breakfast
(on a cold freetown morning)
under the same cotton tree
for years
he wears a gown and coat-of-arms
tattoo on his forehead

he brandishes
rusty metal and stick
his spoon, his weapon,
his only true companion
as he whispers obscenity
at his innermost demon
grimacing and awaiting
his albatross from toroshima island
he reads

Along the Odokoko River

shakespeare, hemmingway, salinger
brutus, achebe and soyinka
and stories about war in burma
he says he killed monroe
and then slept on her grave
over at forrest lawn

he wears the macbeth crown
and then dance the quasimodo dance
while gnawing on chewing stick
and (this time) a blue colored chalk
as he shouts obscenity at the tree
then does the le gendre transformation
over and over again

Kaleidoscope

I took a look in the mirror
yesterday
and I saw you
not myself.
but you

I am a kissi man
born and raised in bengu
a proud fearless hero
I see you.

a madinga warrior
holding the spear once held
by the great sundiata.
I see you.

you chew my head off
and my headless body's roaming
the great wilderness
looking for a place to rest
and then I see you

you gnaw at my flesh
not out of hate
for you're blessed
but I lose my focus

Along the Odokoko River

when you become enraged
yet still I see you

my headless body still roams
looking for a place to go
whether back to salone
the place we all call home
or resting at a stop
I still see you

this mirror so bold
to show me my whole
far from what I have known
or what I have been told

I am a mendeman
a very strong man
I come from tikonko
a faraway land

a reflection of myself
a salone man
a tropical man
bathing in sweat
even after a rainy night

what future do we hold
what love
what band aid to fix the cracks

Ahmed Koroma

that divided us so
the mirror won't go away
(and I still hear the haunting laugh)
the darkness creating a setting
and unlike a silver screen
showing one image at a time

today I am a lokkoh
tomorrow I'm from port loko
A themneh man
A proud themneh man

this mirror has a map
of peoples holding hands
different faces, same people
all in one land

mirror, mirror what have you
to explain to all for this
you told me I'm from gbinti
but yet you laughed at me

"It doesn't matter," said thee
"Go back and look at me
And tell me whom you see
you are from bombali."

"nay sir, I am a vai

Along the Odokoko River

I come from another land
if not for that your curse
I'd break you piece by piece."

"wow see you are in anguish
pray tell, this is the truth
for every man is just
a reflection of the dust."

I swear ne'er to look at thee
for I have seen enough of me
the moon and stars and all
are one in the sight of God

Ahmed Koroma

When the Lights Are Out

Sir
how can we make
our fractured selves whole?

Also
that shadowy figure I see today
that wail and shriek I hear at bay
Is it you returning back to stay
to claim your land and live again

We've seen some intellectuals
with talent and all.

We've seen real talent wasted
at home and abroad.

What love do we show when the lights are out

How much do we care
say it loud and clear

Along the Odokoko River

I sit and Watch

I sit and watch
at mount olympus
when terror comes
to reign so long

I sit and watch
when lions roar
when tigers resist
and pigs bow their heads
in solitariness

I sit and watch
but cannot stay
when pigs betray
the tigers that day

I sit and watch
but cannot talk
when terror comes
and reigns so long

Ahmed Koroma

House of Lords

ridden with potholes, rain and mud
this road will lead to the mountain top
where peddlers toil, where green grass grows,
and school kids walk, on all ten toes

the whiteness of his car contrasts his mind
he's going up there to feed, to dance

a hill overlooking the shanty town
at sea level, manning the ocean front
helplessly, dangerously and neighborly
residing with plasmodium and gambiensi

the house sits flagrantly on the hilltop
with siren blasting as they race beyond

even the temple, kilometers down
below the hill, on the other side
of the recreation field, that peddler's dream
to one day march into the house of greed

he was a good man until he gets to meet
his companieros at the house of lords

Along the Odokoko River

Morning

I listen to the croaking sound of the frogs
from underneath the rocks of worms
after the call for prayer is silenced
as the *ladani* walks away from the minaret
to perform his rakaats

Our metal containers pound on concrete
as I watch the wetness on the cracks
I force a smile and stretch my arms
to greet the new dawn

Ahmed Koroma

Owl

wide-eyed species that hoot at night

so they brought the pots, pans and drums
to chase away the bird that steals
the ailing kid who cries at night

women chanting, derriere exposed
the bird sat tight and gazed at me

drums and pans got louder still
at daylight's peak, the bird took heed
the women, they chased the culprit of doom
to yet another tree

Along the Odokoko River

OF FLOUR AND TEARS

The Act (inferno)

Ahmed Koroma

Solitude

Infandum, regina, iubes renouare dolorem*

he told the story of a man
who refused to sow salt into the sand
but rather fight and die
the residue, the secret abode he dwelled
and all that was left of him
tell the story of bravery
for he was the bird that hovered at night
the protector of a city, the savior
that rescued those that suffered
in the hands of the ungodly
how he endured the plague
but didn't live to tell the tale
three hundred and sixty days
in solitariness
 but his legacy lives on
story of a man, steadfast and gallant
the ultimate sacrifice for a land he loved

*You command me, o queen, to recall the unspeakable sadness. [Aeneas, a Trojan prince, after the Trojan War ended]... Virgil Written 19 B.C.E

Along the Odokoko River

Diamonds and Pearls

she sits calmly besides the river jordan
gazing and mindful, hands akimbo

she doesn't have the stone to show
so she washes her hands
with spittle.

from nazareth to capernaum
(through yadarnet - to the diamond site)
her mind's eye travels wild
she's never seen the pearls
yet still they say it's hers

king of gems that glitter, shine
along the path she takes all night

but the ring on her finger
tells the story of a widow, without gem
in a land full of wealth
a parade of fools, ten moons and gloom
a gem, at best, she only wishes she gets

but the only rock, the one she owns
cleft for her, she hides herself within
away from the mad rumble of dead bones

Ahmed Koroma

At the wall
(Kaibara City, Animal Suffer!)

she is battered and maimed
clipper-fingers forced between
ripping her innocence apart.
for the first time…

the brutal act is unbearable
so she hollers in a vacuum
cries unheard
as the riotous crowd chants:

death to democracy
we killed peace at last
lest it brings more peace
and democracy…

nurture anarchy and chaos
slaughter consciousness and Love
nothingness reigns supreme
in this land of entropy

When Hopes Die

silent wailing, grieving hearts
latent pain, bottled stress
waiting on tomorrow
will it ever come

bare-footed kids and walking canes
side by side in alleyway
dashing toward the morrow
will they stumble and fall

mildewed books and battered brain
empty shells, countless names
gone with tomorrow
will they ever call

joyless rides in countryside
a kidnapped lad who's drugged and high
missing his tomorrow
will he ever come

hostage taking, fire blazin'
from mountain top the land's a-razin'
destroying our tomorrow
will they ever stop

Ahmed Koroma

Betrayal

you betray your core
when you fall all over for
the sugarcoated talk of their wicked bosses

who order massacre upon your land
and spill blood while waving the magic wand

did you not see through swollen eyes
the catastrophe of the night,
as you call God a million times

the unborn child paid with his life
the suckling mother with her arms
silently sobbing on and on
if this is peace then give me war

Blood and Pain

The river flows beneath the camp
water
red with blood and pain
effervescent
intermittently hot and cold
volcanic
but hitherto dormant flow

the redness intensifies by night
the creeping sound of bats and man

gnashing teeth and boot-strapped call
wailing noise, the battle's drawn

friends, foes, sisters, mothers
who do you know, where will you go

heaving hearts, shattered dreams
re-occurring

hate, abyss, more hate
a brotherly malice

this river's been flowing for so long

Ahmed Koroma

Images I: A tragic loss

An *Oro* hollers all through the night
some silent whispering in the dark
a cold chill crawlin' up your spine
(last night I woke up drenched in sweat
I saw a man hung by his neck.)

"O Muse! The causes and the crimes relate"³
what actions 'take what beds to lay
A heap of dirt prepared too late

Those rambling noises awake the dead
an echo streaming through the night

Recurring dream caught in a web
"(A horrid sight!) ev'n in the hero's view,"

The choir hurriedly sings a tune:
'O burnt-out mess, what cherished dream
being replaced by Dante's fling'

Inertness grip the steady flow
once joyous, killed by single blow
(of hate)

What loss; what great loss.
"The Trojans, worn with toils,

Along the Odokoko River

and spent with woes..."
walking, the potholes
alleys and roads

Oh bare-footed men and aimless souls.
aiming to nowhere (and no hopes)
did not your sun come out at night
a blazing torch of bloodstained bright

This fire, set by Satan's men
chalk-faced and groomed in leo's den.
their blood saturates with alkaloid fluid
which oozes out their pores with speed.

What cause this 'mare if not for greed
to kill a man and his offspring.

To reign, (oh my) this pouring rain
won't wash away my endless pain
last night (or was it Sunday night)
my sweet dream ended with a fight

What hater of gladness knocks my door
aft' briefly stop at thirty-four
a ghostly town of constant fear
like those they left far, far behind.

The river stops it flow at night
the rain, a corrugated beat to dance

Ahmed Koroma

"Transfix'd, and naked, on a rock she bound..."
sacrificed to die alone at last

This Gibb's at zero, confusing road.
energy, which way would it flow
'let my people go', oh whither Pharaoh
their hearts, they dealt a vicious blow

Or left to suffer; rebirth at last
when souls are scattered in the wild
bless ye, I still can't see the gain
that brought y'all this very pain

"Approach the chamber, and destroy your sight..."[4]
 unspeakable grief engulfed this land
but the deadly bandits swing and dance
they've lost their way; they've lost their mind.

Images II: A tragic loss

"But, in the palace of the king, appears
A scene more solemn, and a pomp of tears.
Maids, matrons, widows, mix their common moans;
Orphans their sires, and sires lament their sons.
All in that universal sorrow share
And curse the cause of this unhappy war..."

                                      Aeneid

The ripple sound, the town's awake
the yawning of another day
the drizzle resonates with the bay
the sun penetrates its fiery rays

A joyous hope once passing by
hangs by a single thread of rye
but baked and couched in cyanide pan
a wave of hell eclipses this town.

"Against the Tiber's mouth, but far away,
an ancient town was seated on the sea"
until that day when hell broke loose
that sad morning of January sixth

Who would forget, who wouldn't fret
when bliss is killed by drunken fools

Ahmed Koroma

many lives are wasted in this town
many put on hold while Satan frown

"Beneath his frowning forehead lay his eye;
for only one did the vast frame supply...."
drug crazy bellow and chaos sound
hail of bullets reverberate around

The Hasting crier couldn't sing aloud
his trachea clog by viral phlegm
his eyes wide open, he sees it all
the swarm of bees at the gate of hell

"A swarm of bees, that cut the liquid sky,
(unknown from whence they took their airy flight,)"
landed they did at the runaway strip
the town of Hastings in a horror grip

A westward march with axe a-swinging
the bullets grazing', the town's a-waking
the sky is lost, the bees are swarming
oh wretched me, Freetown is dust

The cotton tree could brave the wind
its branches chelat-ing on the mighty trunk
the bees, they circle around this tree
their humming heard at Wilberforce

Along the Odokoko River

A Twisted Metal

I am a twisted metal
the forgotten one
after the fire is ousted
after the rain is gone

I am a twisted metal.
rusted
darkened and bent
malleable and twisted dent

I am a twisted metal
once alloyed and strong
the ever-backbone structure
of a once promising land

I am a twisted metal
left to oxidize in rain
brittle,
with sharpened edges

I am a twisted metal

Ahmed Koroma

The Exchange

I see you gaze, helplessly over yonder
the green turning to red, the fire
I see the emblem on the stick
for once, I don't see me
You warn me this time will come
as you read me Ecclesiastes
behind that wall, bottom of the hill
(where green is now red)
you tell me not to kill
True son, the wind is ne'er overtaken
unless it wants you to
the sacrifice, the prophecy
we preach
is nothing of this breed
What befalls us when time is ceased
and blanket falls over the sea
what prayer say, bending, the wail
that rescue not
ev'n the born-again
Do not despair, do not sin more
nor cast reproach upon your Lord
This is man-made, for
it is those that stray wild
that take a kid and her mother's arms

The Song

The cries of my ancestors re-echo
and the cola-nuts, cowries and blood
spilled into the River Rokel
still continue to flow
The perpetual drumming is heard
melody streaming through the wind
reverberating in the woods
creating a dying yet spirited sound
The drama continue to unfold
little children dancing in the cold
with ornament on the arms
and bells on their toes
The music resonates through the fire
women gyrate in pendulum style
with chalks on charcoal faces
showing the new moon smile
We clap our hands and sing sad songs
clad in frayed piece of woven cloth
battered but strong we will not fall
with worn-out zest we will stand tall
We lost our homes but not our soul
we did not know which way to go
but that solemn humming sound we hear
relieve our hearts and keep us whole
Your place of worship and abode
engulfed in flames and gloomy hope
a deathly dream we cannot cope

Ahmed Koroma

our lives in tattered dangling ropes
But distant ray of hope I see
across the wasteland to the sea
a cherished sight beyond the hills
inflame my heart and comfort me

Along the Odokoko River

OF FLOUR AND TEARS

Aftermath (after the storn)

Ahmed Koroma

*"When it rains here it will
be more than the memory of water
that rises to shatter our houses"*

Immigrants (Highlife for Caliban – Lemuel Johnson)
Nostalgia

Break-neck speed
on elevated roads
splashing
muddy rainwater
on books and sandal toes
a reminder once again it's morning
at sackville street

Drip drip drip...
underneath a corrugated metal roof
awaiting a glimpse of color
from the yet unseen rainbow
my rainbow

It's violet,
the outer color in the sky.
but half-blinded
by passing pajeros
(on those dirt elevated roads)
I still see my rainbow

Along the Odokoko River

Sackville street is dark again
the kerosene lamps are out
and there's mourning
in the morning
long after the rain
long after my rainbow
had disappeared again

The kid in the gutter
his mind once glowing with colors
(of the rainbow)
is now an expert
on kalashnikov and alphajets
What replacement toy
for yesteryear's alphabets

The mother and child
strapped on her back
with colorful *oja,*
balanced on her head
earthenware pot and hole-punched pans
to fetch water

Sackville Street
un-illuminated but full of life
as ever
with *agbara* paralleling the gutter
and the kid
streaming paper boats

Ahmed Koroma

and plastic mammals.

Freetown's wall street merchants
trading tobacco and dollar bills
while we kick football
and play, sing and wish
for rain

The azan
we hear the call for prayer
(but we play, sing and wish
for rain)
five times a day.

What makes the sun
disappear at night
and give way to the moon
What makes the cock crow
and little flowers grow

Sackville Street is bright again
the kerosene lamps are re-flaming
and yes the rain is gone
but can I still see my rainbow
after this bloody storm

Along the Odokoko River

Salioko

He sprinkles millets and tosses goat horns
dead at dawn

And with his umbilical cord fastened tightly
around his neck
he lies prostrate

at the crossroads where four roads meet
where the moon crossed path with the sun
cursing the demons of annihilation
who breathe fire from their nostrils
who carry water for *Firaona**

The dusk that extinguished his life
rekindles
and the sun rises over salioko
once more

(F*iraona – Pharaoh, the political and religious leader of the Egyptian people)*

The trumpet stabbed the night in one last defiant note…
                              --Wole Soyinka

Ahmed Koroma

Forgiveness

As Ogun springs from the body of Yemeja
so is mercy that shower on Salioko
(along the stream where we bathe all night)

we wash our faces with tears of joy
the tears that roll after the mighty storm
the celebration, after the thunderous roar

Ha! Not long ago Ogun wept
the path we traverse was dark and muddy
the moon was red and deprived us,
the radiance of chiefs and the dead

the fire burns the shrub that cures
the path to manhood

for it is annihilation when kin destroy
the bond that fasten them
at the umbilicus

but we catapult

mercy, the town crier roars
as he beats his *ago-go*
as the rain pours at the doorstep of the healer

Along the Odokoko River

Salioko is re-born
peace is heard around the hills

the land where darkness once slept.

Ahmed Koroma

His Return

as darkness spreads over the quiet town
we hear the distant sound of trumpet blaring across the land
and the late wind whispers goodbye
to sorrow

at ile salioko, along the path to the two rivers
(where the battle was lost and won)
we celebrate his return
and dance the hunter's dance,

we paint our faces and collect cowries
a reminder of the sad yesteryears

 but salioko is reborn
(the cry of joy again is heard)
and the newborn now has a name
the one who brought joy
did we shave his head and beat our drums
and throw away the remains of last night's *Sara*
 ah! the image of salioko
The smell of daylight
The smell of joy
kayode is home
again

Along the Odokoko River

The drink of Peace

Sap-filled trees and morning dew
cold feet
tiptoeing into marshy fields
searching for cure.

Silence
except for croaking and bellowing
from awaking toads
greeting the unseen sun

She moves
skillfully dancing her way
one rock to one rock
across the streaming bay

She balances on her head
her mental anguish over this
if herbs could cure it like it did
my abdominal pain last week

So she squeezes
only harder this time
extracting all she could get
the sap from the Cinchona tree

Ahmed Koroma

I move my bed across the room
Trying to catch the night in its flight

--Monologue (Syl-Cheney Coker -- Concerto for an exile)

Isidore on the Yucatan

A pitch-dark night
whistling sound and dancing roofs
and debris sailing through the air

Night bats hang tight, metals melt
for Isidore warns and warms
the heart of those that stray the night

Rain, wind, the palm-oiled
pans from last night's meal
parade the parlor at Isidore's sight

And the peninsula darkness
singing wind rushing past our abode
twice last night

Our roasted tongue and red wide eyes
from tonight's meal
saying goodbye to the night in its flight
And our resting place, on top of rusty nails

Along the Odokoko River

awaiting the rushing stream and Isidore's might

But this night
we drink hot soup for supper
and the music from the raindrop thumps our hearts

The mighty wind blows at a vexing speed
uprooting the Iroko tree on the way out

Ahmed Koroma

Exodus

We threshed wheat by the winepress
our bread baskets
ransacked by fearless hyenas
toppled and left to rot in this barren land
the one we deserted, the one that
smelled of urea

Our finger nails remain blood stained
from the scar of our own blood

The boat spiral in mid-stream
mad voices rant,
clapping hands held high

Hallelujah, home again
(the drumbeat reverberates around the hills)
to this land of great drought
now, the water flows fast uphill
gushing and greeting those who dare
to return

The suckling child who never left
returns to his home

Afterword by

Kayode R. Robbin-Coker, PhD. Cambridge, UK

'*The trial cannot proceed,*' *said the King in a very grave voice,* '*until all the jurymen are back in their proper places-- ALL,*' *he repeated with great emphasis, looking hard at Alice as he said so.*

I trust, Dear Reader, that you will have read the offerings – ALL of them – in this inspired and inspirational collection of Ahmed Koroma's poems, before allowing yourself the risky indulgence of reading these post-engagement ramblings of mine. Beginning at the beginning, going on till you come to the end and then stopping made perfect sense to the King, to Citizen Alice and the White Rabbit alike but it's a logic which, as readers, we sometimes find difficulty following. I should know; I freely confess to a pseudo-Arabic-derived orientation to the printed word which makes the back pages of every other book I pick up a default starting point. I can't always remember what happens afterwards, but I can say with absolute confidence that if I ever wind up on Mastermind I already know what my specialist subject will be: "The Endings of Books I have 'Read' , 1971 – 2011."

T.S.Eliot's somewhat lazy speculation in rather similar circumstances: "After such knowledge, what forgiveness?" comes to mind here; I would suggest that regardless of how you arrived at this page, whether by conscientiously observing letter and spirit of The King's Speech (as aforementioned) or via a more minimalist, perhaps Twitter-inspired reading strategy, you must commit yourself hereafter to making quite a few more (extremely profitable, I assure you) trips back to the body of this collection. Each visit will, I dare say, prompt greater, deeper, better appreciation of the sheer allusive, imaginative, visionary and dialectic breadth of experience and expression that is Ahmed Koroma's Of Flour and Tears.

There is a structural solidity to this collection which may well be purely coincidental, or else an instinctive, almost atavistic synthesis of mens *scientifica* and ars *poetica*. I know which theory I prefer - Ahmed Koroma is, after all, a poet who, as Professor Porter reminds us, combines a natural creativity with the formal training and professional occupation of a Chemist. *Ergo*, Poetry in Potion. The thirty poems are judiciously distributed in a tripartite structure of sections titled "Prelude (the smoke)" – 13 poems, "The Act (inferno)" – 10 poems, and "Aftermath (after the firestorm)" – 7 poems. Notice, if you will, the felicitous yet subtle tapering of the frame - three fewer poems in each succeeding section - towards its terminus which is the playout poem "Exodus".

Thirty poems, then, in three sections. Thirty pieces of silver and a trinity thrown in for good measure? The kind of idle speculation Koroma, born and raised in an Islamic religious tradition, would greet with an enigmatic, non-committal smile. Our shared perspectives over the last decade or so on a range of (in no particular order) religious, cultural, social, historical and political issues as they relate to our country, Sierra Leone, and our continent, Africa, ensure that we are rarely surprised by incongruities. We spent most of our childhood and formative adolescent years (not quite contemporaneously, I hasten to add – there are sound antediluvian, pre-railroadite grounds and reasons for my writing the afterword to *his* book and not the other way round) in the same part of Sierra Leone – the East End of Freetown, where "growing up" was shorthand for heedlessly dashing to and fro across the indistinct frontiers between religions, cultures and languages our parents' generation had laboured to sketch out for us.

It is this casual, confident at-homeness with the totality of that complex experience that is Sierra Leone (or rather "Salone", our colloquial preference) that gives so much of Ahmed Koroma's poetry its authentic, utterly credible ring.

Quite unsurprising, then, that the Prelude poem "The Mad Man" is subtitled "from East End Freetown"? There are only three capitalised words in this poem and they are all in the title, so there's no mistaking the fact that the Mad Man is the star of his own poem. By contrast, a roll call of Koroma's famous antecedents in the trade is deliberately cast in an e. e. cummings-like altered reality (that way Madness lies?):

Ahmed Koroma

he reads
shakespeare, hemmingway, salinger
brutus, achebe and soyinka
and stories about war in burma
he says he killed monroe
and then slept on her grave
over at forrest lawn ...

The titles promise, and the poems deliver. On a purely semantic level it might be argued that there is a predetermined policy of signposting which suggests Koroma is unwilling to trust his reader to make all the required connections unaided. So we get a couple of heavy "no smoke without fire" and "all's well that (sort of) ends well" nudges as we move through *Prelude ... Act ... Aftermath*. But that's as predictable as it got for me. What distinguishes the collection most is the variety of voice and the many moods made manifest as Koroma manages to surprise us by joy, pain, elation, disappointment, courage, hope. I've probably left something out of that list.

I was particularly enthralled by the intensity of vision apparent in the second section of this collection. Koroma's anguished, frantic, narrative voice in this middle passage could have been borrowed from *Death of a Salesman*'s Willie Loman: the woods are burning, for pity's sake, and all we can do is watch them burn. Admittedly, the warning signs are there from the outset and evident in the subtitling (inferno) so the Dantesque tenor of lines such as:

*A cold chill crawlin' up your spine
(Last night I woke up drenched in sweat
I saw a man hung by his neck)...*

*Those rambling noises awake the dead
An echo streaming through the night"*

("Images: A tragic loss")

and "Hostage taking, fire blazin'/from mountain top the land's a-razin'" ("When Hopes Die") was not entirely unexpected. But the title of the first poem in this sequence – "Solitude" – barely hints at the darkness of the experiences to come. The initial reluctance reflected in *"Infandum regina, iubes renovare dolorem"* is soon cast aside as Koroma uses an imaginatively allusive backdrop of Greek tragedy to chronicle, in sometimes excruciatingly painful word pictures, the brutalities and suffering which characterised Salone's savage civil war of 1991 – 2002.

This middle section is like a successful exorcism which clears the way for some positive resolutions. If you are one of those readers who likes poetry to take them to safe places, to provide validations of feel-good experiences and emotions, then you will have probably shaken your head more than once, muttered uneasily from time to time, perhaps even felt like a guest at one of Pound's reading sessions recalling the chilling epigraphic loquitur on Bertans de Born in "Sestina: Altaforte":

"Dante Alighieri put this man in hell for that he was a stirrer up of strife. Eccovi! Judge ye! Have I dug him up again?"

But there are evident, even generous compensations. In a manner not dissimilar to Wordsworth's "Growth of a Poet's Mind" Koroma's journey from "Prelude" to "Aftermath" appears to leave him somewhat positively resolved, in the end, to "grieve not, rather find strength in what remains behind". That certainly appears to be the place we arrive at with the final poems in this collection. There are recurrent images of rebirth and renewal; the sun rising over Salioko is a much more benign elemental force than the Prelude version which
"blinds those that dare to dream/those with zest and fervour, those unafraid to speak".

"Exodus" – reminding us even here at the end that this poet is anything but predictable – turns out to be not about a going out as much as about a coming back in. It opens with a jumble of unpromising, nihilistic images, but gradually transcends those inauspicious beginnings to deliver an unexpectedly upbeat, hope-filled message of homecoming:

Along the Odokoko River

"*Hallelujah, home again,
(the drumbeat reverberates around the hills)*"

There is, admittedly, a residue of the dark in the reference to "this land of great drought" but it is more than adequately balanced out by the rather miraculous if unscientific promise implied in:

*now, the water flows fast uphill
gushing and greeting those who dare
to return*

And who might those intrepid prodigals be? Well, there is only one, solitary figure identified - none other than, apparently:

the suckling child who never left ...

Now who would have staked anything on such outcomes? The fast flowing water promises respite for the land of great drought, and the suckling child encapsulates a hope for the future after the inferno. Thank God, then, for the Aftermath, if not the afterword.